Trusting God
When Life Goes
Wrong

LIFE ON THE EDGE SERIES

Trusting God When Life Goes Wrong

Dr. James Dobson

WORD PUBLISHING

NASHVILLE

A Thomas Nelson Company

TRUSTING GOD WHEN LIFE GOES WRONG

PUBLISHED BY WORD PUBLISHING, NASHVILLE, TENNESSEE.

Unless otherwise indicated, Scripture quotations used in this book are from The Holy Bible, New International Version (NIV). Copyright © 1973, 1978, 1984, International Bible Society. Used by permission of Zondervan Bible Publishers.

Other references are from the following sources:
The King James Version of the Bible (KJV).
The New King James Version (NKJV). Copyright 1979, 1980, 1982, 1990, Thomas Nelson, Inc., Publisher.

LIBRARY OF CONGRESS CATALOGING-IN-PUBLICATION DATA

Dobson, James C., 1936–
    Trusting God when life goes wrong / by James Dobson.
      p. cm. — (Life on the edge series)
   ISBN 0-8499-4276-4
    1. Young adults—Religious life. 2. Trust in God—Christianity. 3. Suffering—Religious aspects—Christianity. I. Title.
BV4529.2 .D67 2001
248.8'3—dc21
                    00-049976
                    CIP

Printed in the United States of America.

00 01 02 03 04 05 PHX 9 8 7 6 5 4 3 2 1

Preface

IF YOU ARE BETWEEN SIXTEEN AND TWENTY-SIX years of age, this series of books is written specifically for you. Others are welcome to read along with us, of course, but the ideas are aimed directly at those moving through what we will call the "critical decade."

Some of the most dramatic and permanent changes in life usually occur during those ten short years. A person is transformed from a kid who's still living at home and eating at the parents' table to a full-fledged adult who should be earning a living and taking complete charge of his or her life. Most of the decisions that will shape the next fifty years will be made in this era, including the choice of an occupation, perhaps the decision to marry, and the establishment of values and principles by which life will be governed.

I recall pondering these questions in my youth and thinking how helpful it would be to talk with someone who had a few answers—someone who understood what I was facing. But like most of my friends, I never asked for help.

What makes this period even more significant is the impact of early mistakes and errors in judgment. They can undermine all that is to follow. A bricklayer knows he must be very careful to get his foundation absolutely straight; any wobble in the bricks at the bottom will create an even greater tilt as the wall goes up. So it is in life.

In this series of books, we'll talk about how to interpret the will of God and recognize His purposes for you, the task of thinking through the challenges you are facing, and how you will accomplish your life goals. A contractor would never begin a skyscraper without detailed architectural and engineering plans to guide his or her work. Likewise, persons in the critical decade between age sixteen and twenty-six owe it to their future to figure out who they are and what they want out of life. Helping you do that is what this book is all about.

—Dr. James Dobson

Introduction

IN PHILIPPIANS 4:7, THE APOSTLE PAUL WRITES: "Rejoice in the Lord always, I will say it again: Rejoice!"

Sounds impossible sometimes, doesn't it? It can be hard to rejoice during times when it seems like your whole world is crumbling around you. When difficult times come, do you sometimes find yourself questioning God? When we lose a loved one, or break up with the person we had hoped to marry, or get turned down for a job that we *really* wanted, it can be very easy for us to become bitter and angry at God. *Why me?* we ask ourselves. *I've played by the rules and I still got the shaft. Why didn't God answer my prayers?*

It is during these moments when your faith is tested. Will it be refined by fire or will it melt away? The Lord has said, "Trust me." But do we, especially when we don't get what we want? In *Trusting God When Life Goes Wrong*, Dr. James Dobson discusses how tragedies and rough times affect our spiritual lives. Sharing his own experiences when things have not worked out as planned, he explains the importance of trusting God—even when what He is doing makes no sense to us. Dr. Dobson will help you to see the bigger picture in God's plan for your life and how trusting Him during the difficult times will strengthen your faith to go the distance to your eternal reward in heaven.

Contents

1   When Life Goes Wrong

AS YOU LIVE LIFE ON THE EDGE, GOD CAN HELP you remain steady when hardships and stresses challenge you—but you must trust God when life goes wrong. In my book *When God Doesn't Make Sense,* I discuss our inability to explain everything He is doing in our lives, especially when the storm clouds gather.

For example, Chuck Frye was a bright young man of seventeen, academically gifted and highly motivated. After graduating near the top of his class in high school, he went on to college, where he continued to excel in his studies. Upon completion of his bachelor's of science degree, he applied for admittance to several medical schools.

The competition for acceptance into medical school was, and is, fierce. At the time, I was a professor at the University of Southern California School of Medicine, where only 106 students were admitted each year out of 6,000 applicants. That was typical of accredited medical programs in that era. Despite these long odds, Chuck was accepted at the University of Arizona School of Medicine, and he began his formal training.

During that first term, Chuck was thinking about the call of God on his life. He began to feel that he should forego high-tech medicine in some lucrative setting in favor of service on a foreign field. This eventually became his definite plan for the future. Toward the end of that first year of training, however, Chuck was not feeling well. He began experiencing a strange and persistent fatigue. He made an appointment for an examination in May and was soon diagnosed with acute leukemia. By November Chuck Frye was dead.

How could Chuck's heartsick parents then, and how can we now, make sense of this incomprehensible act of God? This young man loved Jesus Christ with all his heart and sought only to do His will. Why was he taken in his prime despite many agonized prayers for his healing by godly family members and faithful friends? The Lord clearly said "No" to them all. But why?

Thousands of young doctors complete their education every year and enter the medical profession, some for less-than-admirable reasons. A tiny minority plan to spend their professional lives with the down-and-outers of the world. But here was a marvelous exception. If permitted to live, Chuck could have treated thousands of poor and needy people who otherwise would have suffered and died in utter hopelessness. Not only could he have ministered to their physical needs, but his ultimate desire was to share the gospel with those who had never heard this greatest of stories. Thus, his death simply made no sense.

Visualize with me the many desperately ill people Dr. Chuck Frye might have touched in his lifetime, some with cancer, some with tuberculosis, some with congenital disorders, and some being children too young to even understand their pain. Why would divine Providence deny them his dedicated service?

There is another dimension to the Frye story that completes the picture. Chuck became engaged to be married in March of that first year in medical school. His fianceé was named Karen Ernst, who was also a committed believer in Jesus Christ. She learned of Chuck's terminal illness six weeks after their engagement, but she chose to go through with their wedding plans. They became husband and wife less than four months before his tragic death. Karen then enrolled in medical school at the University of Arizona and after graduation became a medical missionary in Swaziland, South Africa. Dr. Karen Frye served there in a church-sponsored hospital until

1992. I'm sure she wonders—amidst so much suffering—why her brilliant young husband was not allowed to fulfill his mission as her medical colleague. And yes, I wonder, too.

The great theologians of the world can contemplate for the next fifty years the dilemma posed by Chuck Frye's death, but they are not likely to produce a satisfying explanation. God's purpose in this young man's demise is a mystery, and there it must remain. Why, after much prayer, was Chuck granted admittance to medical school if he could not live to complete his training? From whence came the missions call to which he responded? Why was so much talent invested in a young man who would not be able to use it? And why was life abbreviated in such a mature and promising student, while many drug addicts, winos, and evil-doers survive into old age as burdens on society? These troubling questions are much easier to pose than to answer. And . . . there are many others.

ALL WE CAN ASK IS "WHY?"

The Lord has not yet revealed His reasons for permitting the plane crash that took the lives of my four friends in 1987. They were among the finest Christian gentlemen I have ever known. Hugo Schoellkopf was an entrepreneur and an extremely able member of the board of directors for Focus on the Family. George Clark was a bank president and a giant of a man. Dr. Trevor Mabrey was a gifted surgeon who performed nearly half of his operations at no charge to his patients. He was a soft touch for anyone with a financial need. And Creath Davis was a minister and author who was loved by thousands. They were close friends who met regularly to study the Word and assure mutual accountability for what they were learning. I loved these four men. I had been with them the night before that last flight, when their twin-engine plane went down in the Absaroka mountain range in Wyoming. There were no survivors. Now, their precious wives and children are left to struggle on alone.

Why? What purpose was served by their tragic loss? Why are Hugo and Gail's two sons, the youngest of the children among the four families, deprived of the influence of their wise and compassionate father during their formative years? I don't know, although the Lord has given Gail sufficient wisdom and strength to carry on alone.

At the first mention of the "awesome why," I think also of our respected friends Jerry and Mary White. Dr. White is president of the Navigators, a worldwide organization dedicated to knowing Christ and making Him known. The Whites are wonderful people who love the Lord and live by the dictates of

Scripture. But they have already had their share of suffering. Their son Steve drove a taxi for several months while seeking a career in broadcasting. But he would never achieve his dream. Steve was murdered by a deranged passenger late one night in the usually quiet city of Colorado Springs.

> *Human worth does not depend on beauty, intelligence, or accomplishments. We are all more valuable than the possessions of the entire world simply because God gave us that value. This fact remains true, even if every other person on earth treats us like losers.*
>
> *Thirty-eight Values to Live By*
> —Dr. James Dobson

The killer was a known felon and drug abuser who had a long history of criminal activity. When he was apprehended, the police learned that he had called for the cab with the intent of shooting whoever arrived to pick him up. Any number of drivers might have responded. Steve White took the call. It was random brutality, beyond any rhyme or reason. And it occurred within a family that had honored and served God for years in full-time Christian service.

Further examples of inexplicable sorrows and difficulties could fill the shelves of the world's largest library, and every person on earth could contribute illustrations of his own. Wars, famines, diseases, natural disasters, and untimely deaths are never easy to rationalize. But large-scale miseries of this nature are sometimes less troubling

> *Why would God permit this to happen to me!? It is a question every believer—and many pagans—have struggled to answer.*

to the individual than the circumstances that confront each of us personally. Cancer, kidney failure, heart disease, sudden infant death syndrome, cerebral palsy, Down syndrome, divorce, rape, loneliness, rejection, failure, infertility, widowhood—these and a million other sources of human suffering produce inevitable questions that trouble the soul. Why would God permit this to happen to me!? It is a question every believer—and many pagans—have struggled to answer. And contrary to Christian teachings in some circles, the Lord typically does not rush in to explain what He is doing.

2 | The Sovereignty of God

IF YOU BELIEVE GOD IS OBLIGATED TO EXPLAIN Himself to us, you ought to examine the Scripture. Solomon wrote in Proverbs 25:2, "It is the glory of God to conceal a matter. . . ." Isaiah 45:15 states, "Truly you are a God who hides himself." First Corinthians 2:11 says, "No one knows the thoughts of God except the Spirit of God." Deuteronomy 29:29 reads, "The secret things belong to the LORD our God" (NKJV). Ecclesiastes 11:5 proclaims, "As you do not know the path of the wind, or how the body is formed in a mother's womb, so you cannot understand the work of God, the Maker of all things." Isaiah 55:8–9 teaches, "'For my thoughts are not your thoughts, neither are your ways my ways,' declares the Lord. 'As the heavens are higher than the earth, so are my ways higher than your ways and my thoughts than your thoughts.'"

Clearly, Scripture tells us we lack the capacity to

grasp God's infinite mind or the way He intervenes in our lives. How arrogant of us to think otherwise. Trying to analyze His omnipotence is like an amoeba attempting to comprehend the behavior of man. Romans 11:33 (NKJV) indicates that God's judgments are "unsearchable" and His ways "past finding out!" Similar language is found in 1 Corinthians 2:16: "Who has known the mind of the LORD that he may instruct him?" Clearly, unless the Lord chooses to explain Himself to us, which He does not often do, His motivation and purposes are beyond the reach of mortal man.

Scripture tells us we lack the capacity to grasp God's infinite mind or the way He intervenes in our lives.

What this means in practical terms is that many of our questions—especially those that begin with the word *why*—will have to remain unanswered for the time being.

The apostle Paul referred to the problem of unanswered questions when he wrote, "Now we see but a poor reflection; then we shall see face to face. Now I know in part; then I shall know fully, even as I am fully known" (1 Cor. 13:12). Paul was explaining that we will not have the total picture until we meet in eternity, and by implication, we must learn to accept that partial understanding.

GOD'S WONDERFUL PLAN?

Unfortunately, many believers do not know that there will be times in every person's life when circumstances don't add up—when God doesn't appear to make sense. This aspect of the Christian faith is not well advertised. We tend to teach new Christians the portions of our theology that are attractive to a secular mind. For example, Campus Crusade for Christ (an evangelistic ministry I respect highly) has distributed millions of booklets called "The Four Spiritual Laws." The first of those scriptural principles states, "God loves you and offers a wonderful plan for your life." That statement is certainly true. However, it implies that a believer will always comprehend the "wonderful plan" and that he or she will approve of it. That may not be true.

For some people, such as Joni Eareckson Tada, the "wonderful plan" means life in a wheelchair as a quadriplegic. For others it means early death, poverty, or the scorn of society. For the prophet Jeremiah, it meant being cast into a dark dungeon. For other Bible characters it meant execution. Even in the most terrible of circumstances, however, God's plan is "wonderful" because anything in harmony with His will ultimately "works for the good of those who love him, who have been called according to his purpose" (Rom. 8:28).

Still, it is not difficult to understand how confusion can develop at this point, especially for those of you who are young. During the springtime of your years, when health is good and the hardships, failures, and sorrows have not yet blown through your tranquil world, it is relatively easy to fit the pieces in place. You can honestly believe, with good evidence, that it will always be so. At that point, however, you are extremely vulnerable to spiritual confusion.

> *There will be times in every person's life when circumstances don't add up.*

Dr. Richard Selzer is a surgeon and a favorite author of mine. He writes the most beautiful and compassionate descriptions of his patients and the human dramas they confront. In his book *Letters to a Young Doctor,* he said that most young people seem to be protected for a time by an imaginary membrane that shields them from horror. They walk in it every day but are hardly aware of its presence.

As the immune system protects the human body from the unseen threat of harmful bacteria, so this mythical membrane guards them from life-threatening situations. Not every young person has this protection, of course, because children do die. But most of them are shielded—and don't realize it. Then one day the membrane tears, and horror seeps into a person's life or into the life of a loved one. It is at this moment that an unexpected theological crisis presents itself.

NO GREATER LOVE

So what am I suggesting—that our heavenly Father is uncaring or unconcerned about His vulnerable sons and daughters, that He taunts us mere mortals as some sort of cruel, cosmic joke? It is almost blasphemous to write such nonsense. Every description given to us in Scripture depicts God as infinitely loving and kind, watching over His earthly children tenderly and guiding the steps of the faithful. He speaks of us as "his people, the sheep of his pasture" (Ps. 100:3). This great love led Him to send His only begotten Son as a sacrifice for our sin that we might escape the punishment we deserve. He did this because He "so loved the world" (John 3:16).

The apostle Paul expressed it this way: "For I am convinced that neither death nor life, neither angels nor demons, neither the present nor the future, nor any powers, neither height nor depth, nor anything

13

else in all creation, will be able to separate us from the love of God that is in Christ Jesus our Lord" (Rom. 8:38–39). Isaiah conveyed this message to us directly from the heart of the Father: "So do not fear, for I am with you; do not be dismayed, for I am your God. I will strengthen you and help you; I will uphold you with my righteous right hand" (Isa. 41:10). No, the problem here is not with the love and mercy of God.

One of the most breathtaking concepts in all of Scripture is the revelation that God knows each of us personally and that we are in His mind both day and night. There is simply no way to comprehend the full implications of this love by the King of kings and Lord of lords. He is all-powerful and all-knowing, majestic and holy, from everlasting to everlasting. Why would He care about us—about our needs, our welfare, our fears? We have been discussing situations in which God doesn't make sense. His concern for us mere mortals is the most inexplicable of all.

Not only is the Lord "mindful" of each one of us, but He describes Himself throughout Scripture as our Father. In Luke 11:13 we read, "If you then, though you are evil, know how to give good gifts to your children, how much more will your Father in heaven give the Holy Spirit to those who ask him!" Psalm 103:13 says, "As a father has compassion on his children, so the Lord has compassion on those who fear him." But on the other hand, He is likened to a mother in Isaiah 66:13: "As a mother comforts her child, so will I comfort you."

A FATHER'S LOVE

Being a parent of two children, both now grown, I can identify with these parental analogies. They help me begin to comprehend how God feels about us. If necessary, Shirley and I would give our lives for Danae and Ryan in a heartbeat. We pray for them every day, and they are never very far from our thoughts. And how vulnerable we are to their pain! Can it be that God actually loves His human family infinitely more than we, "being evil," can express to our own flesh and blood? That's what the Word teaches.

An incident occurred during our son's early childhood that illustrated for me this profound love of the heavenly Father. Ryan had a terrible ear infection when he was three years old that kept him (and us) awake most of the night. Shirley bundled up the toddler the next morning and took him to see the pediatrician. This doctor was an older man with very little patience for squirming kids. He wasn't overly fond of parents, either.

After examining Ryan, the doctor told Shirley that the infection had adhered itself to the eardrum and could only be treated by pulling the scab loose with a wicked little instrument. He warned that the procedure would hurt and instructed Shirley to hold her son tightly on the table. Not only did this news alarm her, but enough of it was understood by Ryan to send him into orbit. (It didn't take much to do that in those days.)

Shirley did the best she could. She put Ryan on the examining table and attempted to hold him down. But he would have none of it. When the doctor inserted the pick-like instrument in his ear, the child broke loose and screamed to high heaven. The pediatrician then became angry at Shirley and told her if she couldn't follow instructions she'd have to go get her husband. I was in the neighborhood and quickly came to the examining room. After hearing what was needed, I swallowed hard and wrapped my 200-pound, six-foot-two-inch frame around the toddler. It was one of the toughest moments in my career as a parent.

What made it so emotional was the long mirror Ryan was facing as he lay on the examining table. This made it possible for him to look directly at me as he screamed for mercy. I really believe I was in greater agony in that moment than was my terrified little boy. It was too much. I turned him loose—and got a beefed-up version of the same bawling-out Shirley had received a few minutes earlier. Finally, however, the grouchy pediatrician and I finished the task.

I reflected later on what I was feeling when Ryan was going through so much suffering. What hurt me was the look on his face. Though he was screaming and couldn't speak, he was "talking" to me with those big blue eyes. He was saying, "Daddy! Why are you doing this to me? I thought you loved me. I never thought you would do anything like this! How could you? Please, please! Stop hurting me!"

It was impossible to explain to Ryan that his suffering was necessary for his own good—that I was trying to help him—that it was love that required me to hold him on the table. How could I tell him of my compassion in that moment? I would gladly have taken his place on the table, if possible. But in his immature mind, I was a traitor who had callously abandoned him.

Then I realized there must be times when God also feels our intense pain and suffers along with us. Wouldn't that be characteristic of a Father whose love is infinite? How He must hurt when we say in confusion, "How could You do this terrible thing, Lord? Why me? I thought I could trust You! I thought You were my friend!" How can He make us understand, with our human limitations, that our agony is necessary—that it does have a purpose— that there are answers to the tragedies of life? I wonder if He anticipates the day when He can make us understand what was occurring in our time of trial. I wonder if He broods over our sorrows.

Some readers might doubt that an omnipotent God with no weaknesses and no needs is vulnerable to this kind of vicarious suffering. No one can be certain. We do know that Jesus experienced the broad range of human emotions and that He told Philip, "Anyone who has seen me has seen the Father" (John 14:9). Remember that Jesus was "deeply moved in spirit and troubled" when Mary wept over Lazarus. He also wept as He looked over the city of Jerusalem and spoke of the sorrow that would soon come upon the Jewish people. Likewise, we are told that the Spirit intercedes for us now with "groans that words cannot express" (Rom. 8:26). It seems logical to assume, therefore, that God the Father is passionately concerned about His human "family" and shares our grief in those unspeakable moments "when sorrows like sea billows roll." I believe He does.

3 | Brace Yourself, and Be Prepared

THE REASON I HAVE CHOSEN TO INCLUDE THIS discussion in *Life on the Edge* is to help brace you, my younger readers, for those difficult times that will invade your lives sooner or later. It is inevitable. In my work with families who are going through these hardships, from sickness and death to marital conflict and financial distress, I have found it common for those in crisis to feel great frustration with God. This is particularly true when things happen that seem illogical and inconsistent with what had been taught or understood. Then if the Lord does not rescue them from the circumstances in which they are embroiled, their frustration quickly deteriorates into anger and a sense of abandonment. Finally, disillusionment sets in, and their spirits begin to wither.

This can even occur in very young children who are vulnerable to feelings of rejection from God. I'm reminded of a boy named Chris whose face had been burned in a fire. He sent this note to his psychotherapist:

> *Dear Dr. Gardner,*
>
> *Some big person, it was a boy about 13, he called me a turtle. And I know he said this because of my plastic surgery. And I think God hates me because of my lip. And when I die, he'll probably send me to hell.*
>
> Love, Chris

Chris naturally concluded that his deformity was evidence of God's rejection. It is a logical deduction in the eyes of a child: If God is all powerful and He knows everything, then why would He let such a terrible thing happen to me? He must hate me. Unfortunately, Chris is not alone. Many others come to believe the same satanic lie. In fact, the majority of us will someday, at some time, feel a similar alienation from God. Why? Because those who live long enough will eventually be confronted by happenings they will not understand. That is the human condition.

The great danger for people who have experienced this kind of disillusionment is that Satan will use their pain to make them feel victimized by God. What a deadly trap that is! When a person begins to conclude that he or she is disliked or hated by the Almighty, demoralization is not far behind.

TRIALS ARE NOTHING NEW

If you have begun to slide into that kind of despair, it is extremely important to take a new look at Scripture and recognize that you are not unique in the trials you face. All of the biblical writers, including the giants of the faith, went through similar hardships. Look at the experience of Joseph, one of the patriarchs of the Old Testament. His entire life was in shambles. He was hated by his brothers, who considered killing him before agreeing instead to sell him as a slave. While in Egypt, he was imprisoned, falsely accused by Potiphar's wife of attempted rape, and threatened with execution. There is no indication that God explained to Joseph what He was doing through those many years of heartache or how the pieces would eventually fit together. He had no way of knowing that he would eventually enjoy a triumphal reunion with his family. He was expected, as you and I are, to live out his life one day at a time in something less than complete understanding. What pleased God was Joseph's faithfulness when nothing made sense.

Let's zip over to the New Testament and look at the disciples and other early Christian leaders. Jesus said there was no greater man born of woman than John the Baptist, but this honored Christian pioneer soon found himself in Herod's stinking dungeon. There an evil woman named Herodias had him beheaded because he had condemned her immoral conduct. There is no record in Scripture that an angel visited John's cell to explain the meaning of his persecution. This great, godly man who was the designated forerunner to Jesus went through the same confusing experiences as we. It is comforting to know that John responded in a very human way. He sent a secret message to Jesus from his prison cell, asking, "Are you the one who was to come, or should we expect someone else?"(Matt. 11:2). Have you ever felt like asking that question?

Look at the martyrdom of Stephen, who was stoned to death for proclaiming the name of Christ, and the disciple James, of whom the twelfth chapter of Acts devotes only one verse: "He [King Herod Agrippa] had James, the brother of John, put to death with a sword" (Acts 12:2). Tradition tells us that ten of the twelve disciples were eventually executed (excluding Judas, who committed suicide, and John, who was exiled). We also believe that Paul, who was persecuted, stoned, and flogged, was later beheaded in a Roman prison. The second half of the eleventh chapter of Hebrews describes some of those who suffered for the name of Christ:

Others were tortured and refused to be released, so that they might gain a better resurrection. Some faced jeers and flogging, while still others were chained and put in prison. They were stoned; they were sawed in two; they were put to death by the sword. They went about in sheepskins and goatskins, destitute, persecuted and mistreated—the world is not worthy of them. They wandered in deserts and mountains and in caves and holes in the ground. These were all commended for their faith, yet none of them received what had been promised. (vv. 35–39)

What pleased God was Joseph's faithfulness when nothing made sense.

Read that last verse again. Note that these saints lived in anticipation of a promise that had not been fulfilled by the time of their deaths. A full explanation never came. They had only their faith to hold them steady in their time of persecution. The Life Application Bible commentary says of this chapter, "These verses summarize the lives of other great men and women of faith. Some experienced outstanding victories, even over the threat of death. But others were severely mistreated, tortured, and even killed. Having a steadfast faith in God does not guarantee a happy, carefree life. On the contrary, our faith almost guarantees us some form of abuse from the world. While we are on earth, we may never see the purpose of our suffering. But we know that God will keep his promises to us." That is precisely the point.

Few of us are called upon to lay down our lives like those heroes of the early church, but modern-day examples do exist. Reverend Bill Hybels shared an experience in his book *Too Busy Not To Pray* that speaks dramatically to this issue:

There is no record in Scripture that an angel visited John's cell to explain the meaning of his persecution.

A couple of years ago, a member of my church's vocal team and I were invited by a Christian leader named Yesu to go to southern India. There we joined a team of people from various parts of the U. S. We were told that God would use us to reach Muslims and Hindus and nonreligious people for Christ. We all felt called by God to go, but none of us knew what to expect.

When we arrived, Yesu met us and invited us to his home. Over the course of the next few days, he told us about his ministry.

Yesu's father, a dynamic leader and speaker, had started the mission in a Hindu-dominated area. One day a Hindu leader came to Yesu's father and asked for prayer. Eager to pray with him, hoping he would lead him to Christ, he took him into a private room, knelt down with him, closed his eyes and began to pray. While he was praying, the Hindu man reached into his robe, pulled out a knife and stabbed him repeatedly.

Yesu, hearing his father's screams, ran to help him. He held him in his arms as blood poured out onto the floor of the hut. Three days later, his father died. On his deathbed he said to his son, "Please tell that man that he is forgiven. Care for your mother and carry on this ministry. Do whatever it takes to win people to Christ."

What an inspiring and humbling story! It makes me feel ashamed for complaining about the petty problems and frustrations I have encountered through the years. Someday, the Lord may require a similar sacrifice of me in the cause of Christ. If so, I pray I will have the courage to accept whatever His will is for me. Untold multitudes have dedicated their lives to His service in this manner.

So tell me, where did we get the notion that the Christian life is a piece of cake? Where is the evidence for the "name it, claim it" theology that promises God will skip along in front of us with His great cosmic broom, sweeping aside each trial and every troubling uncertainty? To the contrary, Jesus told His disciples that they should anticipate suffering. He said, "I have told you these things, so that in me you may have peace. In this world you will have trouble. But take heart! I have overcome the world" (John 16:33). Paul wrote, "In all our troubles my joy knows no bounds. For when we came into Macedonia, this body of ours had no rest, but we were harassed at every turn—conflicts on the outside, fears within" (2 Cor. 7:4–5). Peter left no doubt about difficulties in this Christian life when he wrote, "Dear friends, do not be surprised at the painful trial you are suffering, as though something strange were happening to you. But rejoice that you participate in the sufferings of Christ, so that you may be overjoyed when his glory is revealed" (1 Pet. 4:12–13). Note in each of these references the coexistence of both joy and pain.

> *With God, even when nothing is happening . . . something is happening.*
>
> *Thirty-eight Values to Live By*
> —Dr. James Dobson

This is the consistent, unequivocal expectation we have been given by the biblical writers, and yet we seem determined to rewrite the text. That makes us sitting ducks for satanic mischief.

My concern is that many believers apparently feel God owes them smooth sailing or at least a full explanation (and perhaps an apology) for the hardships they encounter. We must never forget that He, after all, is God. He is majestic and holy and sovereign. He is accountable to no one. He is not an errand boy who chases the assignments we dole out. He is not a genie who pops out of the bottle to satisfy our whims. He is not our servant—we are His. And our reason for existence is to glorify and honor Him.

Even so, sometimes He performs mighty miracles on our behalf. Sometimes He chooses to explain His actions in our lives. Sometimes His presence is as real as if we had encountered Him face to face. But at other times when nothing makes sense—when what we are going through is "not fair"—when we feel all alone in God's waiting room—He simply says, "Trust Me!"

Does this mean we are destined to be depressed and victimized by the circumstances of our lives? Certainly not. Paul said we are "more than conquerors." He wrote in Philippians 4:4–7, "Rejoice in the Lord always. I will say it again: Rejoice! Let your gentleness be evident to all. The Lord is near. Do not be anxious about anything, but in everything, by prayer and petition, with thanksgiving, present your requests to God. And the peace of God, which transcends all understanding, will guard your hearts and minds in Christ Jesus."

Clearly, what we have in Scripture is a paradox. On the one hand we are told to expect suffering and hardship that could even cost us our lives. On the other hand, we are encouraged to be joyful, thankful, and "of good cheer." How do those contradictory ideas link together? How can we be triumphant and under intense pressure at the same time? How can we be secure when surrounded by insecurity? That is a mystery, which, according to Paul, "transcends all understanding."

For those of you out there today who have already been through hard times and are desperate for a word of encouragement, let me assure you that you can trust this Lord of heaven and earth. Remember that Scripture warns us to "lean not on your own understanding" (Prov. 3:5).

Note that we are not prohibited from trying to understand. I've spent a lifetime attempting to get a handle on some of the imponderables of life. But we are specifically told not to lean on our ability to make the pieces fit. "Leaning" refers to the panicky demand for answers—throwing faith to the wind if a satisfactory response cannot be produced. It is pressing God to explain Himself—or else! That is where everything starts to unravel.

If we can comprehend even a tiny portion of the Lord's majesty and the depth of His love for us, we can deal with those times when He defies human logic and sensibilities. Indeed, that is what we must do. Expect confusing experiences to occur along the way, and don't be dismayed when they arrive. Welcome them as friends—as opportunities for your faith to grow. Hold fast to your faith, without which it is impossible to please Him. "Lean into the pain" when your time to suffer comes around. Never yield to feelings of self-pity or victimization, which are Satan's most effective tools against us. Instead, store away your questions for a lengthy conversation in eternity, and then press on toward the mark. Any other approach is foolhardy.

> *Where did we get the notion that the Christian life is a piece of cake?*

4 Answering the Eternal Questions

ONE OF MY PROFESSIONAL COLLEAGUES DIED toward the end of my final year on the staff of Children's Hospital of Los Angeles. He had served on our university medical faculty for more than twenty-five years. During his tenure as a professor, he had earned the respect and admiration of both professionals and patients, especially for his research findings and contribution to medical knowledge. This doctor had reached the pinnacle of success in his chosen field and enjoyed the status and financial rewards that accompany such accomplishment. He had tasted every good thing, at least by the standards of the world.

At the next staff meeting following his death, a five-minute eulogy was read by a member of his department. Then the chairman invited the entire staff to stand, as is our custom in situations of this nature, for one minute of silence in memory of the fallen colleague. I have no idea what the other members of the staff thought about during that sixty-second pause, but I can tell you what was going through my mind.

I was thinking, *Lord, is this what it all comes down to? We sweat and worry and labor to achieve a place in life, to impress our fellow men with our competence. We take ourselves so seriously, overreacting to the insignificant events of each passing day. Then finally, even for the brightest among us, all these successes fade into history and our lives are summarized with a five-minute eulogy and sixty seconds of silence. It hardly seems worth the effort, Lord.*

But I was also struck by the collective inadequacy of that faculty to deal with the questions raised by our friend's death. Where had he gone? Would he live again? Will we see him on the other side? Why was he born? Were his deeds observed and recorded by a loving God? Is that God interested in me? Is there a purpose to life beyond investigative research and professorships and expensive automobiles? The silent response by 250 learned men and women seemed to symbolize our inability to cope with those issues.

Well, how about it? Do you know where you stand on the fundamental issues posed by the death of my friend? More to the point, have you resolved them for yourself and for those you love? If not, then I hope you'll read on. We will address those questions and the search for life's ultimate meaning and purpose.

It is a matter of incredible significance. Until we know who we are and why we are here, no amount of success, fame, money, or pleasure will provide much satisfaction. Until we get a fix on the "big picture," nothing will make much sense.

> *Satan will attempt to offer you whatever you hunger for, whether it be money, power, sex, or prestige. But Jesus said, "Blessed are those who hunger and thirst for righteousness" (Matt. 5:6).*
>
> *Thirty-eight Values to Live By*
> —Dr. James Dobson

It is so important to pause and think through some of these basic issues while you are young, before the pressures of job and family become distracting. Everyone must deal with the eternal questions sooner or later. You will benefit, I think, from doing that work now. Whether you are an atheist, a Muslim, a Buddhist, a Jew, a New-Ager, an agnostic, or a Christian, the questions confronting the human family are the same. Only the answers will differ.

5 | Life: What's It All About?

Millions of people acknowledge today that they do not know the meaning of life. Indeed, sociologists tell us that a desperate search for spiritual truth is underway throughout Western cultures. Baby boomers have been seeking something to believe in for almost three decades. In the 1970s, they were involved in a quest that came to be known as "the discovery of personhood." It motivated some of them to participate in nude counseling, transcendental meditation, reincarnation and other Eastern mysticism, ESP, astrology, psychoanalysis, therapeutic massage, far-out theologies, and a seminar on the self called EST.

The quest for personhood failed miserably. Indeed, most people came out of these programs more confused and frustrated than before. They looked for the answers to life's questions within themselves and were inevitably disappointed. Here's why.

When I was four years old, I was digging in the

yard and discovered a bed of onions my aunt had planted that spring. Not knowing what they were, I began trying to peel them. As I tore away the outer layer, I found another shiny one tucked underneath. When that one was stripped away, yet another lay below. The onion just got smaller and smaller as I clawed at its structure. My aunt was shocked a few minutes later to find fragments of her prized onions spread all over the lawn.

Human beings are like those onions in some ways. When you strip away all the layers one by one, not much remains to "discover." You will never find real meaning among your selfish interests, feelings, and aspirations. The answers do not lie within you. In fact, the more you promote yourself, the emptier you feel.

Jesus addressed that precise issue when He said, "If any man will come after me, let him deny himself, and take up his cross daily, and follow me. For whosoever will save his life shall lose it: but whosoever will lose his life for my sake, the same shall save it" (Luke 9:23–24 KJV). In other words, meaning and purpose will be found outside—not inside—the onion.

Where will you find answers to the major questions of life? How will you identify the values that moth and rust will not corrupt and thieves cannot break in and steal? All of us are faced with those questions. How can they be answered?

THE BREVITY OF LIFE

It might be useful to engage in a mental exercise I call the "end-of-life test." Project yourself many years down the road when your time on earth is drawing to a close. That may seem morbid to you at such a young age, but the brevity of life is a very important biblical concept. The psalmist David said our lives are like the flowers of the field that blossom in the morning and then fade away (see Ps. 103:15–16). Moses expressed the same idea in Psalm 90 when he wrote, "Teach us to number our days" (v. 12 KJV). What the biblical writers were telling us is that we're just passing through. At best, we're merely short-termers on this planet.

Given this understanding of the brevity of life, I invite you to imagine yourself as an old man or woman looking back across many decades. Think about the highlights and treasures of the past seventy or eighty years. What kinds of memories will be the most precious to you in that final hour?

I may be in a position to help answer those questions because I've had to deal with them. It began on a basketball court a few years ago. At fifty-four years of age, I thought I was in great physical condition. I had recently undergone a medical examination and was pronounced to be in excellent health. I could play basketball all day with men twenty-five years my junior. But there were unpleasant surprises in store for me on that particular morning.

As I went in for a lay-up, I was seized by a pain in the center of my chest. It was unlike anything I'd ever experienced. I excused myself, telling my friends I didn't feel well. Then I drove to a nearby emergency clinic. Incidentally, this was the same hospital where my dad was taken after suffering a massive heart attack twenty-one years earlier. So began ten days that would change my life.

For a man who thought of himself as "Joe College," it was a shock to realize that I might be dying. It took awhile for that thought to sink in. But about ten hours later, an enzyme report confirmed that I had had a heart attack. Nurses came at me from every direction. Tubes and IVs were strung all over me. An automatic blood pressure machine pumped frantically on my arm throughout the night, and a supervising nurse delicately suggested that I not move unless absolutely necessary. That does tend to get your attention.

As I lay there in the darkness listening to the beep-beep-beep of my heart on the oscilloscope, I began to think very clearly about what really mattered in my life. As I've said, encountering death has a way of jerking your priorities into line. Everything fluffy and insignificant falls away, and the true values begin to shine like burnished gold. I knew that I was ready to go if the Lord should beckon me across the great divide. I had lived my life so as to be prepared for such a time as that, but I didn't expect it to come so quickly.

Fortunately for me, the damage to my heart proved to be minor, and God has restored me to vigorous health. I exercise every day, and I'm eating some of the finest birdseed money can buy. Still, that scary experience in the hospital made an indelible impression on me and gave me a new zest for life.

WHEN EVERYTHING IS ON THE LINE

That's why I have a good notion of how you're likely to react when your time comes around. Ask yourself what you will care about when everything is on the line. Will it be the businesses you created and nourished? Will it be the plaques that hang on the wall? Will it be the academic degrees you earned from prestigious universities? Will it be the fortune you accumulated? Will it be the speeches you gave, the paintings you produced, or the songs you sang? Will it be the books you wrote or the offices to which you were elected? Will it be the power and influence you held? Will it be a five-minute eulogy and sixty seconds of silence after you're gone? I doubt it.

Achievements and the promise of posthumous

acclaim will bring some satisfaction, no doubt. But your highest priorities will be drawn from another source. When all is said and done and the books are closing on your life, I believe your treasures will lie much closer to home. Your most precious memories will focus on those you loved, those who loved you, and what you did together in the service of the Lord. Those are the basics. Nothing else will survive the scrutiny of time.

To elaborate on that concept, let me take you back to that gymnasium where my heart attack occurred. Two years earlier, another highly significant event had occurred just a few feet from where I was stricken. My friends and I played basketball three times a week on that court, and on that particular morning, we had invited Pete Maravich to join us.

It was an audacious thing to do. "Pistol Pete," as he was dubbed by the media, had been one of the greatest basketball players of all times. He was the Michael Jordan or the Magic Johnson of his day. He set more than forty NCAA college records at Louisiana State University, many of which still stand. He had averaged forty-four points per game during his three years at LSU. After graduation, Pete was drafted by the National Basketball Association and became the first player ever to receive a million-dollar contract. When he retired because of knee problems, he was elected to the NBA Hall of Fame the first year he was eligible. There is very little that can be done with a basketball that Pete Maravich didn't accomplish.

So for a bunch of "duffers" to invite a superstar like Pete to play with us took some gall, even though he was forty years old at the time. To our delight, he agreed to come and showed up at 7 A.M. I quickly learned that he had been suffering from an unidentified pain in his right shoulder for many months. Aside from playing in the NBA "Legends Game," which was televised nationally, Pete had not been on a basketball court in more than a year. Nevertheless, we had a good time that morning. Pete moved at about one-third his normal speed, and the rest of us huffed and puffed to keep up. We played for about forty-five minutes and then took a break to get a drink. Pete and I stayed on the court and talked while waiting for the other players to come back.

"You can't give up this game, Pete," I said. "It has meant too much to you through the years."

"You know, I've loved playing this morning," he replied. "I really do want to get back to this kind of recreational basketball. But it wouldn't have been possible in the last few months. The pain in my shoulder has been so intense that I couldn't have lifted a two-pound ball over my head."

"How are you feeling today?" I asked.

"I feel great," he said.

PETE'S LAST WORDS

Those were Pete's last words. I turned to walk away, and for some reason I looked back in time to see him go down. His face and body hit the boards hard. Still, I thought he was teasing. Pete had a great sense of humor, and I assumed that he was playing off his final comment about feeling good.

I hurried over to where Pete lay and still expected him to get up laughing. But then I saw that he was having a seizure. I held his tongue to keep his air passage open and called for the other guys to come help me. The seizure lasted about twenty seconds, and then Pete stopped breathing. We started CPR immediately but were never able to get another heartbeat or another breath. Pistol Pete Maravich, one of the world's greatest athletes, died there in my arms at forty years of age.

Several of us accompanied the ambulance to the hospital, where we prayerfully watched the emergency room staff try to revive Pete for about forty-five minutes. But it was no use. He had left this earth, and there was nothing anyone could do to bring him back.

An autopsy revealed a few days later that Pete had a congenital malformation of the heart and never knew it. That was why his shoulder had been hurting. Whereas most of us have two coronary arterial systems that wrap around the heart, Pete only had one. How he was able to do such incredible exploits on the basketball court for so many years is a medical mystery. He was destined to drop dead at a fairly young age, and only God knows why it happened during the brief moment when his path crossed mine.

The shock of Pete's untimely death is impossible to describe. None of the men who witnessed the tragedy will ever forget it. My heart goes out to his lovely wife, Jackie, and their two sons, Jason and Joshua. I spoke at his funeral three days later and still feel a bond of friendship with his little family.

It is important to know something about Pete's background to understand who he was. Quite frankly, he had been a troublemaker when he was younger. He was a heavy drinker who broke all the rules. His attitude deteriorated in the NBA, and he finally quit in a huff. This man who had received every acclaim that can come to an athlete hit the skids emotionally. After retirement, he stayed in his house day after day to avoid autograph-seeking fans and because he had nowhere to go. There he sat, depressed and angry, for two years.

Something incredible happened at that crucial moment in Pete's life. He was in bed one night when he heard someone speak his name. He sat upright, wondering if he had been dreaming. Then he heard the voice again. Pete realized that God was calling him. He immediately knelt beside his bed and gave his heart to the Lord. It was a total consecration of his mind, body, and soul.

For the last five years of his life, all he wanted to talk about was what Jesus Christ had done for him. He told that story to reporters, to coaches, to fans, and to anyone who would listen. The day Pete died, he was wearing a T-shirt that bore the inscription, "Looking unto Jesus."

I was able to share that testimony with the media, which took it around the world within an hour. "You think Pete's great love was basketball," I told them, "but that was not his passion. All he really cared about was Jesus Christ and what He had done in Pete's life." And now I'm relaying that message to you. Perhaps that is why the Lord placed this good man in my arms as his life ebbed away.

6 Be There!

NOW I NEED TO TELL YOU SOMETHING HIGHLY personal that happened next. I went home and sat down with our son, Ryan, who was seventeen years old at the time. I asked to talk to him about something of extreme importance to us both.

I said, "Ryan, I want you to understand what has happened here. Pete's death was not an unusual tragedy that has happened to only one man and his family. We all must face death sooner or later and in one way or another. This is the 'human condition.' It comes too early for some people and too late for others. But no one will escape, ultimately. And, of course, it will also happen to you and me. So without being morbid about it, I want you to begin to prepare yourself for that time.

"Sooner or later, you'll get the kind of phone call that Mrs. Maravich received today. It could occur ten or fifteen years from now, or it could come tomorrow.

But when that time comes, there is one thought I want to leave with you. I don't know if I'll have an opportunity to give you my 'last words' then, so let me express them to you right now. Freeze-frame this moment in your mind, and hold on to it for the rest of your life. My message to you is Be there! Be there to meet your mother and me in heaven. We will be looking for you on that resurrection morning. Don't let anything deter you from keeping that appointment.

> *Pete had a congenital malformation of the heart and never knew it.*

"Because I am fifty-one years old and you are only seventeen, as many as fifty years could pass from the time of my death to yours. That's a long time to remember. But you can be sure that I will be searching for you just inside the Eastern Gate. This is the only thing of real significance in your life. I care what you accomplish in the years to come, and I hope you make good use of the great potential the Lord has given to you. But above every other purpose and goal, the only thing that really matters is that you determine now to be there!"

That message is not only the most valuable legacy I could leave to Ryan and his sister, Danae. It is also the heart and soul of what I have tried to convey in this series. Be there! This must be our ultimate objective in living. Within that two-word phrase are answers to all the other questions we have posed.

Jesus Christ is the source—the only source—of meaning in life. He provides the only satisfactory explanation for why we're here and where we're going. Because of this good news, the final heartbeat for the Christian is not the mysterious conclusion to a meaningless existence. It is, rather, the grand beginning to a life that will never end.

> *Faith in God is like believing a man can walk over Niagara Falls on a tightrope while pushing a wheelbarrow. Trust in God is like getting in the wheelbarrow! To believe God can do something miraculous is one thing; to risk His willingness to do it in your life is another.*
>
> *Thirty-eight Values to Live By*
> —Dr. James Dobson

That same Lord is waiting to embrace and forgive anyone who comes to Him in humility and repentance. He is calling your name, just as He called the name of Pete Maravich. His promise of eternal life offers the only hope for humanity. If you have never met this Jesus, I suggest that you seek spiritual counsel from a Christian leader who can offer guidance. You can also write to me, if that would help.

If our paths don't cross this side of heaven, I'll be looking for you in that eternal city. By all means, Be there!

Thanks for reading along with me. I hope to meet you someday. If our paths don't cross this side of heaven, I'll be looking for you in that eternal city. By all means, Be there!

PORTIONS OF THIS SERIES OF BOOKS HAVE BEEN previously published in other books by James Dobson. The author is grateful to these publishers for permission to reprint from these volumes:

Thirty-eight Values to Live By, Word Publishing, 2000.

Life on the Edge: A Young Adult's Guide to a Meaningful Future, Word Publishing, 1995.

Dr. Dobson Answers Your Questions, Tyndale House Publishers, 1988.

Emotions: Can You Trust Them? Regal Books, 1984.

Hide or Seek, Fleming H. Revell Company, 1974, 1990.

Love for a Lifetime, Multnomah, 1987.

Love Must Be Tough, Word Publishing, 1983.

Parenting Isn't for Cowards, Word Publishing, 1987.

Preparing for Adolescence, Regal Books, 1980, 1989.

The Strong-Willed Child, Tyndale House Publishers, 1978.

Straight Talk to Men and Their Wives, Word Publishing, 1980.

What Wives Wish Their Husbands Knew about Women, Tyndale House Publishers, 1975.

When God Doesn't Make Sense, Tyndale House Publishers, 1993.

About the Author

DR. JAMES DOBSON is founder and president of Focus on the Family, a non-profit evangelical organization dedicated to the preservation of the home. He is recognized as one of America's foremost authorities on the family and is the author of numerous books, including *The New Dare to Discipline, The Strong-Willed Child, When God Doesn't Make Sense, Love Must Be Tough, Straight Talk to Men, Parenting Isn't for Cowards,* and *Life on the Edge: A Young Adult's Guide to a Meaningful Future.* Dr. Dobson is a licensed psychologist in the state of California and a licensed marriage, family and child therapist in the state of Colorado. He was formerly an assistant professor of pediatrics at the University of Southern California School of Medicine. His international radio broadcast, *Focus on the Family,* is heard on more than four thousand stations worldwide. He and his wife, Shirley, are the parents of two young adult children, Ryan and Danae.

dditional books in the *Life on the Edge* Series:

Adapted from the best-selling book, *Life on the Edge*, these
seven pocket-sized booklets offer insight and advice for a
generation searching for significance. Additional books in
this series cover such topics as:

emotions
love
money
compatibility
God's will
parents
life's ironies

 WORD PUBLISHING
www.wordpublishing.com